Mediterranean Diet Cookbook for Two

Perfectly Portioned and Balanced Recipes with Mediterranean Flavors

Alan Caplan

LEGAL & DISCLAIMER

The information contained in this book and its contents is not designed to replace or take the place of any form of medical or professional advice; and is not meant to replace the need for independent medical, financial, legal, or other professional advice or services, as may be required. The content and information in this book has been provided for educational and entertainment purposes only.

The content and information contained in this book has been compiled from sources deemed reliable, and it is accurate to the best of the Author's knowledge, information, and belief. However, the Author cannot guarantee its accuracy and validity and cannot be held liable for any errors and/or omissions. Further, changes are periodically made to this book as and when needed. Where appropriate and/or necessary, you must consult a professional (including but not limited to your doctor, attorney, financial advisor, or such other professional advisor) before using any of the suggested remedies, techniques, or information in this book.

Upon using the contents and information contained in this book, you agree to hold harmless the Author from and against any damages, costs, and expenses, including any legal fees potentially resulting from the application of any of the information provided by this book. This disclaimer applies to any loss, damages or injury caused by the use and application, whether directly or indirectly, of any advice or information presented, whether for breach of contract, tort, negligence, personal injury, criminal intent, or under any other cause of action. You agree to accept all risks of using the information presented inside this book.

You agree that by continuing to read this book, where appropriate and/or necessary, you shall consult a professional (including but not limited to your doctor, attorney, or financial advisor or such other advisor as needed) before using any of the suggested remedies, techniques, or information in this book.

Table Of Contents

Introduction

The Mediterranean diet is more than just a way of eating; it is a lifestyle rooted in centuries of tradition. Inspired by the dietary patterns of countries bordering the Mediterranean Sea, such as Greece, Italy, and Spain, this diet is known for its emphasis on whole, natural foods that nourish both the body and mind.

Why Choose the Mediterranean Diet?

Numerous studies have shown that the Mediterranean diet is one of the healthiest ways to eat. It has been linked to a lower risk of heart disease, improved brain function, and even longevity. Unlike restrictive diets that focus on eliminating entire food groups, the Mediterranean diet is a balanced approach that promotes fresh, nutrient-dense ingredients.

Unlike fad diets that come and go, the Mediterranean diet is backed by decades of scientific research. The combination of fresh vegetables, lean proteins, whole grains, and healthy fats provides essential nutrients that support overall well-being. Additionally, it is not just about what you eat but also about how you eat—enjoying meals with family, savoring flavors, and embracing a slower, more mindful approach to food.

Health Benefits

One of the primary reasons people adopt the Mediterranean diet is for its incredible health benefits. Rich in antioxidants, healthy fats, and fiber, this diet helps reduce inflammation, supports heart health, and maintains stable blood sugar levels. Additionally, it has been associated with a reduced risk of neurodegenerative diseases, making it an excellent choice for long-term wellness.

Adapting the Mediterranean Diet for Two

Cooking for two can be both enjoyable and rewarding, and the Mediterranean diet makes it easy to create delicious, wholesome meals without excess waste. Whether you are a couple looking to eat healthier together or simply want to simplify meal prep, this book provides recipes and tips to help you make the most of Mediterranean-inspired cuisine for two.

In the following chapters, we will explore the fundamentals of the Mediterranean diet, its key ingredients, and a variety of delicious, easy-to-make recipes tailored for two people. Get ready to embark on a flavorful journey toward better health!

The Mediterranean Diet Fundamentals

The Mediterranean diet is not just a way of eating but a holistic approach to health that emphasizes fresh, whole foods, mindful eating, and an active lifestyle. Rooted in the culinary traditions of countries bordering the Mediterranean Sea, this diet promotes long-term well-being through a balanced intake of nutrients and flavors.

Core Principles of the Mediterranean Diet

The Mediterranean diet revolves around a few fundamental principles that make it both delicious and sustainable. These principles focus on natural, nutrient-rich foods, simple cooking methods, and an emphasis on enjoying meals with loved ones.

Prioritize Fresh and Seasonal Produce

Fruits and vegetables are the foundation of the Mediterranean diet. They provide essential vitamins, minerals, fiber, and antioxidants that support overall health. Fresh, seasonal produce not only enhances flavor but also ensures that meals are packed with nutrients. Common vegetables include tomatoes, zucchini, bell peppers, spinach, and eggplant, while fruits like oranges, berries, figs, and grapes are regularly consumed.

Emphasize Healthy Fats

Unlike low-fat diets, the Mediterranean diet encourages the consumption of healthy fats, primarily from olive oil, nuts, seeds, and avocados. Extra virgin olive oil is a staple, used for cooking, dressing salads, and drizzling over dishes for extra flavor and nutrition. These fats help reduce inflammation and support heart and brain health.

Whole Grains Over Refined Grains

Whole grains provide essential fiber and nutrients that aid digestion and help maintain stable blood sugar levels. Instead of white bread and refined pasta, the Mediterranean diet includes whole grains such as quinoa, bulgur, farro, brown rice, and whole wheat bread. These grains add texture and depth to meals while keeping them nutritionally balanced.

Dairy in Moderation

Dairy products, particularly Greek yogurt and cheeses like feta and ricotta, are consumed in small portions. These provide calcium, probiotics, and protein while keeping meals light and digestible.

Lean Proteins with a Focus on Fish

Protein sources in the Mediterranean diet come mainly from fish, poultry, legumes, and nuts. Fatty fish like salmon, sardines, and mackerel are rich in omega-3 fatty acids, which support cardiovascular and cognitive health. While red meat is not excluded, it is eaten in moderation, often replaced by plant-based proteins like lentils, chickpeas, and beans.

Herbs and Spices Instead of Excess Salt

Flavor is key in Mediterranean cuisine, but instead of relying on salt, dishes are enhanced with fresh herbs and spices. Basil, oregano, rosemary, thyme, garlic, and lemon are commonly used to elevate flavors while offering additional health benefits, such as anti-inflammatory properties and improved digestion.

Wine in Moderation

A moderate intake of red wine is often associated with the Mediterranean diet, typically enjoyed with meals. However, consumption should be balanced and optional, as excessive alcohol intake can negate the diet's benefits.

Mindful and Social Eating

One of the unique aspects of the Mediterranean diet is its focus on enjoying food as a shared experience. Meals are often eaten slowly, with an emphasis on social connection, which can improve digestion and promote better eating habits.

Foods to Include

The Mediterranean diet is based on whole, unprocessed foods that provide optimal nourishment. Below is a breakdown of recommended food groups:

- Vegetables: Tomatoes, leafy greens, bell peppers, onions, cucumbers, and artichokes.
- Fruits: Berries, oranges, grapes, apples, figs, and melons.
- Whole Grains: Brown rice, quinoa, whole wheat bread, bulgur, and oats.
- Healthy Fats: Extra virgin olive oil, avocados, nuts (almonds, walnuts), and seeds (chia, flaxseeds).
- Protein Sources: Fatty fish (salmon, sardines, trout), poultry, eggs, legumes, beans, and lentils.
- Dairy (in moderation): Greek yogurt, feta cheese, and ricotta.
- Beverages: Water, herbal teas, and moderate amounts of red wine (optional).

Foods to Limit or Avoid

To fully embrace the Mediterranean lifestyle, it is best to limit or avoid overly processed and artificial foods. These include:

- Refined Grains: White bread, pastries, and processed cereals.
- Sugary Beverages: Sodas, energy drinks, and flavored juices.
- Processed Meats: Sausages, hot dogs, and deli meats with preservatives.
- Unhealthy Fats: Margarine, butter, and trans fats found in fried foods.
- Excess Salt and Artificial Ingredients: Packaged and canned foods high in sodium and preservatives.

Adapting the Mediterranean Diet for Two

Cooking for two on the Mediterranean diet can be both practical and enjoyable. Here are some simple strategies to make meal planning easier:

Plan Your Meals Together: Deciding on weekly meals in advance can help reduce food waste and make grocery shopping more efficient.

Batch Cooking and Leftovers: Preparing larger portions of staple foods like grains and roasted vegetables can save time and provide quick meal options.

Portion Control: Cooking for two means finding the right balance to avoid excess leftovers while still enjoying variety.

Experiment with Flavors: Trying new herbs, spices, and ingredient combinations can keep meals exciting and flavorful.

Cook Together: Preparing meals as a team can make the experience more enjoyable and encourage healthier habits.

By following these guidelines, you can create satisfying, wholesome meals that align with the Mediterranean diet while catering to a lifestyle for two. In the next chapter, we will explore the specific health benefits of this diet, including its impact on heart health, weight management, and longevity.

Health Benefits of the Mediterranean Diet for Two

The Mediterranean diet is widely recognized as one of the healthiest ways to eat, offering numerous benefits for both body and mind. Whether you and your partner are looking to lose weight, improve heart health, boost brain function, or simply maintain overall well-being, this lifestyle provides a balanced and sustainable approach to nutrition. Additionally, when combined with an active and mindful lifestyle, the Mediterranean diet helps cultivate long-term health and happiness for couples who choose to embark on this journey together.

Health Benefits of the Mediterranean Diet

Following the Mediterranean diet as a couple can bring numerous health advantages, including:

Weight Loss and Metabolism Support – This diet naturally promotes sustainable weight loss through whole, nutrient-dense foods, healthy fats that keep you full, balanced portion sizes, and gradual, long-lasting results.

Heart Health and Longevity – The Mediterranean diet reduces the risk of heart disease and stroke by emphasizing heart-healthy fats, antioxidants, and whole foods while limiting processed foods and excess sodium.

Brain Function and Cognitive Health – Omega-3 fatty acids, antioxidants, and stable blood sugar levels support brain function, reducing the risk of cognitive decline and improving mood balance.

Anti-Inflammatory Effects – The diet's high intake of fresh fruits, vegetables, nuts, and olive oil helps fight inflammation, lowering the risk of chronic diseases like arthritis and diabetes.

Digestive Health – Fiber-rich foods such as whole grains, legumes, and fresh produce aid digestion and promote gut health.

Balanced Blood Sugar and Diabetes Prevention – The diet's reliance on whole grains, lean proteins, and healthy fats helps maintain stable blood sugar levels, reducing the risk of type 2 diabetes.

Lifestyle Habits for a Healthier Life

The Mediterranean diet is most effective when combined with an active and mindful lifestyle. Here are some key habits to incorporate for a well-rounded approach to health:

Cook and Eat Together

Preparing meals as a couple fosters a deeper connection and encourages healthy eating habits. Cooking at home allows you to choose high-quality ingredients and control portion sizes.

Stay Active

The Mediterranean lifestyle includes daily movement, but it doesn't require intense workouts. Simple activities like walking together, biking, hiking, or practicing yoga can help maintain a healthy weight and improve overall fitness.

Practice Mindful Eating

Enjoying meals slowly, savoring flavors, and paying attention to hunger and fullness cues can prevent overeating and enhance digestion. Avoid eating in front of screens and instead focus on conversation and the dining experience.

Prioritize Sleep and Stress Management

A well-balanced lifestyle includes quality sleep and stress reduction. Practicing relaxation techniques, spending time in nature, and maintaining a consistent sleep schedule all contribute to better health.

Foster Social Connections

Sharing meals with friends, family, or each other strengthens emotional bonds and enhances happiness. The Mediterranean way of life values togetherness, which can have lasting benefits on both physical and mental health.

The Mediterranean diet is more than just a way to eat—it's a lifestyle that promotes weight loss, heart health, brain function, and overall well-being. When adopted as a couple, it becomes a shared journey toward better health, strengthening not just your bodies but also your relationship. By embracing wholesome foods, mindful eating, and an active lifestyle, you and your partner can enjoy a healthier, more vibrant life together.

Now, let's move on to a delightful collection of Mediterranean recipes designed specifically for two!

BREAKFAST RECIPES

This section presents a thoughtfully curated collection of Mediterranean Diet recipes, designed to be both flavorful and nutritious while supporting overall health and well-being. Each recipe is tailored for two, making it easy to enjoy wholesome meals together. Feel free to adjust ingredients to match your tastes and dietary preferences. If you have specific health concerns or dietary restrictions, consulting a healthcare professional or dietitian can help ensure your meals align with your nutritional goals. Embrace the Mediterranean way of eating and enjoy this delicious journey to better health—one shared meal at a time!

Broccoli and Feta Frittata

Cooking Difficulty: 2/10	Cooking Time: 28 minutes	Servings: 2

INGREDIENTS

- 4 large eggs
- 1/4 cup unsweetened almond milk
- 1 cup broccoli florets, chopped
- 1/4 cup red bell pepper, diced
- 1/4 cup cherry tomatoes, halved
- 1/4 cup crumbled feta cheese
- 1/2 teaspoon dried oregano
- 1/4 teaspoon salt
- 1/4 teaspoon black pepper
- 1 tablespoon extra virgin olive oil

DESCRIPTION

STEP 1

Preheat the oven to 375°F (190°C). In a bowl, whisk the eggs, milk, salt, pepper, and oregano until well combined.

STEP 2

Heat olive oil in an oven-safe skillet over medium heat. Add the broccoli and red bell pepper, cooking for 3–4 minutes until slightly softened. Add the cherry tomatoes and stir for another minute. Pour the egg mixture over the vegetables and sprinkle the crumbled feta on top.

STEP 3

Cook for 2–3 minutes on the stovetop until the edges start to set, then transfer the skillet to the oven. Bake for 12–15 minutes, or until the frittata is fully set and slightly golden on top. Let it cool for a minute before slicing and serving.

NUTRITIONAL INFORMATION

220 Calories, 14g Fat, 8g Carbs, 14g Protein

Veggie Breakfast Hash

Cooking Difficulty: 1/10	Cooking Time: 14 minutes	Servings: 2

INGREDIENTS

- 1 medium zucchini, sliced into rounds and quartered
- 1/2 red bell pepper, diced
- 1/2 yellow bell pepper, diced
- 1 small red onion, diced
- 1 tablespoon extra virgin olive oil
- 1/2 teaspoon dried oregano
- 1/4 teaspoon smoked paprika
- salt and black pepper to taste
- 2 slices whole-grain ciabatta, toasted

DESCRIPTION

STEP 1

Heat olive oil in a skillet, add veggies, and sauté for 5-7 minutes until tender. иSeason with oregano, smoked paprika, salt, and pepper. Serve the veggie hash with toasted ciabatta.

NUTRITIONAL INFORMATION

280 Calories, 16g Fat, 32g Carbs, 8g Protein

Oat Pancakes

Cooking Difficulty: 1/10	Cooking Time: 15 minutes	Servings: 2

INGREDIENTS

- ½ cup rolled oats (blended into flour)
- 1 large egg
- ¼ cup almond milk
- ½ teaspoon baking powder
- ½ teaspoon cinnamon
- ½ teaspoon vanilla extract
- 1 teaspoon olive oil (for cooking)
- ¼ cup fresh berries

DESCRIPTION

STEP 1

In a bowl, mix oat flour, baking powder, and cinnamon. Whisk in the egg, almond milk, and vanilla. Heat olive oil in a pan over medium heat. Pour small amounts of batter and cook for 2–3 minutes per side until golden. Serve topped with berries.

NUTRITIONAL INFORMATION

220 Calories, 9g Fat, 32g Carbs, 6g Protein

Mediterranean Sardine Sandwich

Cooking Difficulty: 2/10	Cooking Time: 15 minutes	Servings: 2

INGREDIENTS

- 1 can (4 oz) sardines in olive oil, drained and flaked
- 1/2 avocado, mashed
- 1/4 cup cherry tomatoes, diced
- 1/4 small red onion, finely chopped
- 1 tablespoon extra virgin olive oil
- 1 teaspoon lemon juice
- 1/2 teaspoon Dijon mustard (optional, for extra flavor)
- 1/4 teaspoon dried oregano
- salt and black pepper to taste
- 4 slices whole-grain or sourdough bread, toasted
- 2 large romaine lettuce leaves

DESCRIPTION

STEP 1

In a bowl, mix the flaked sardines, mashed avocado, cherry tomatoes, red onion, olive oil, lemon juice, mustard, oregano, salt, and black pepper until well combined.

STEP 2

Brush one side of each slice of bread with extra virgin olive oil. Heat a skillet over medium heat. Place two slices of bread, oiled side down, in the pan.

STEP 3

Lay a romaine lettuce leaf on each slice, then evenly spread the sardine mixture over the lettuce. Top with the remaining bread slices, oiled side up. Cook for 2–3 minutes on each side until the bread is golden brown and crispy. Remove from heat, slice in half, and serve immediately.

NUTRITIONAL INFORMATION

380 Calories, 20g Fat, 30g Carbs, 22g Protein

Raspberry Chia Pudding

Cooking Difficulty: 1/10	Cooking Time: 5 minutes	Servings: 2

INGREDIENTS

- 1 cup unsweetened almond milk
- 1/4 cup chia seeds
- 1/2 teaspoon vanilla extract
- 1/2 cup fresh raspberries (half mashed, half for topping)
- 1 tablespoon honey or maple syrup (optional)
- 1/4 cup whole-grain granola

DESCRIPTION

STEP 1

Mix almond milk, chia seeds, vanilla, mashed raspberries, and honey (if using). Stir well. Refrigerate for at least 4 hours or overnight, stirring once after 30 minutes. Divide into bowls, top with granola and fresh raspberries, and serve.

NUTRITIONAL INFORMATION

220 Calories, 9g Fat, 30g Carbs, 6g Protein

Mediterranean Shakshuka

Cooking Difficulty: 1/10	Cooking Time: 17 minutes	Servings: 2

INGREDIENTS

- 1 tablespoon extra virgin olive oil
- 1/2 red bell pepper, diced
- 1/2 small red onion, chopped
- 2 garlic cloves, minced
- 1 1/2 cups canned crushed tomatoes
- 1/2 teaspoon ground cumin
- salt and black pepper to taste
- 4 large eggs
- fresh parsley for garnish

DESCRIPTION

STEP 1

Sauté bell pepper, onion, and garlic in olive oil for 3 minutes. Add tomatoes, spices, salt, and pepper. Simmer for 5 minutes. Crack eggs into the sauce, cover, and cook for 5–7 minutes. Garnish with parsley and serve warm.

NUTRITIONAL INFORMATION

280 Calories, 18g Fat, 16g Carbs, 18g Protein

Spiced Spinach & White Bean Toast

Cooking Difficulty: 2/10	Cooking Time: 17 minutes	Servings: 2

INGREDIENTS

- 4 slices whole-grain or sourdough bread
- 1 tablespoon extra virgin olive oil (plus extra for drizzling)
- 1 garlic clove, minced
- 2 cups fresh spinach, chopped
- 1/2 cup canned white beans, drained and rinsed
- 1/2 teaspoon ground cumin
- 1/4 teaspoon smoked paprika
- 1/4 teaspoon dried oregano
- 1 teaspoon lemon juice
- salt and black pepper to taste
- 1/4 teaspoon red pepper flakes (optional)
- 2 tablespoons crumbled feta cheese (optional)

DESCRIPTION

STEP 1

Heat olive oil in a skillet over medium heat. Add the garlic and sauté for about 30 seconds until fragrant. Add the spinach and cook for 2–3 minutes until wilted.

STEP 2

Stir in the white beans, cumin, smoked paprika, oregano, salt, black pepper, and red pepper flakes (if using). Cook for another 2 minutes, stirring occasionally. Remove from heat and add lemon juice, stirring to combine.

STEP 3

Toast the bread slices until golden brown. Spoon the warm spinach and bean mixture over the toasted bread. Drizzle with a little extra virgin olive oil and sprinkle with crumbled feta cheese if desired. Serve!

NUTRITIONAL INFORMATION

330 Calories, 12g Fat, 40g Carbs, 12g Protein

Blueberry Oatmeal Muffins

Cooking Difficulty: 1/10	Cooking Time: 20 minutes	Servings: 2

INGREDIENTS

- ½ cup rolled oats (blended into flour)
- 1 large egg
- ¼ cup unsweetened almond milk
- 1 tablespoon olive oil
- ½ teaspoon baking powder
- ½ teaspoon cinnamon
- 1 teaspoon honey (optional)
- ¼ cup fresh blueberries

DESCRIPTION

STEP 1

Preheat oven to 350°F (175°C). Mix all ingredients in a bowl until smooth. Fold in blueberries. Divide batter into a greased muffin tin. Bake for 15 minutes or until golden. Let cool and enjoy!

NUTRITIONAL INFORMATION

120 Calories, 5g Fat, 15g Carbs, 4g Protein

Apple Cinnamon Oatmeal

Cooking Difficulty: 1/10	Cooking Time: 15 minutes	Servings: 2

INGREDIENTS

- ½ cup rolled oats
- 1 cup unsweetened almond milk
- ½ apple (diced)
- ½ teaspoon cinnamon
- 1 teaspoon honey (optional)
- 1 tablespoon chopped walnuts (for topping)

DESCRIPTION

STEP 1

Preheat oven to 350°F (175°C). In two ramekins, combine oats, almond milk, diced apple, and cinnamon. Stir well. Bake for 10 minutes, or until the oats are tender. Top with walnuts and honey (if using), then serve warm. A simple, comforting, and nutritious breakfast!

NUTRITIONAL INFORMATION

220 Calories, 9g Fat, 30g Carbs, 6g Protein

Eggs with Asparagus & Mushrooms

Cooking Difficulty: 2/10	Cooking Time: 14 minutes	Servings: 2

INGREDIENTS

- 4 large eggs
- 1/2 cup asparagus, trimmed and cut into 1-inch pieces
- 1/4 cup leek, thinly sliced
- 1/4 cup red onion, finely chopped
- 1/2 cup oyster mushrooms, sliced
- 1 tablespoon extra virgin olive oil
- 1/4 teaspoon dried thyme
- salt and black pepper to taste
- 1 tablespoon crumbled feta cheese (optional)

DESCRIPTION

STEP 1

Heat olive oil in a large skillet over medium heat. Add asparagus, leeks, red onion, and mushrooms. Sauté for about 5 minutes until tender. Season with thyme, salt, and black pepper.

STEP 2

Push the vegetables to the sides of the skillet, creating space in the center. Crack the eggs into the skillet and cook to your preferred doneness—about 3–4 minutes for sunny-side-up or longer if you prefer firmer yolks.

STEP 3

Once the eggs are cooked, remove from heat. Sprinkle with crumbled feta if desired. Serve immediately, either as is or with whole-grain toast on the side.

NUTRITIONAL INFORMATION

280 Calories, 18g Fat, 9g Carbs, 18g Protein

Apple Pancakes

Cooking Difficulty: 2/10	Cooking Time: 27 minutes	Servings: 2

INGREDIENTS

- 1 medium apple, grated
- 1/2 cup whole wheat flour
- 1/2 tsp baking powder
- 1/2 tsp cinnamon
- 1/2 cup unsweetened almond milk
- 1 large egg
- 1 tsp honey (optional)
- 1/2 tsp vanilla extract
- 1 tbsp extra virgin olive oil (for cooking)

DESCRIPTION

STEP 1

Mix flour, baking powder, and cinnamon. In another bowl, whisk egg, milk, honey, and vanilla. Combine with grated apple. Heat olive oil in a skillet. Cook pancakes for 2–3 minutes per side until golden. Serve warm, optionally topped with yogurt or nuts.

NUTRITIONAL INFORMATION

220 Calories, 7g Fat, 30g Carbs, 7g Protein

Veggie Omelet Wrap

Cooking Difficulty: 2/10	Cooking Time: 12 minutes	Servings: 2

INGREDIENTS

- 4 large eggs
- 2 tbsp unsweetened almond milk
- salt and black pepper to taste
- 1 tbsp extra virgin olive oil
- 1/2 cup mushrooms, sliced
- 1/2 avocado, diced
- 1/4 cup crumbled feta cheese
- 1/4 cup fresh greens (spinach or arugula)

DESCRIPTION

STEP 1

Whisk eggs, almond milk, salt, and pepper. Sauté mushrooms in olive oil for 3 minutes. Set aside. Pour eggs into the pan, cook until set, then add mushrooms, avocado, greens, and feta on one side. Fold the omelet over like a pocket and cook for another minute. Serve warm.

NUTRITIONAL INFORMATION

310 Calories, 24g Fat, 8g Carbs, 18g Protein

Zucchini and Tomato Frittata

Cooking Difficulty: 2/10	Cooking Time: 25 minutes	Servings: 2

INGREDIENTS

- 2 large eggs
- ¼ cup unsweetened almond milk (or low-fat milk)
- ½ small zucchini (thinly sliced)
- ½ cup cherry tomatoes (halved)
- ¼ small onion (finely chopped)
- 1 tablespoon olive oil
- ¼ teaspoon garlic powder
- ¼ teaspoon black pepper
- ⅛ teaspoon salt
- ¼ teaspoon dried oregano
- 1 tablespoon crumbled feta cheese (optional)
- 2–3 fresh basil leaves (torn, for garnish)

DESCRIPTION

STEP 1

Preheat oven to 375°F (190°C). In an oven-safe skillet, heat olive oil over medium heat. Add onions and zucchini, cooking for 3–4 minutes until soft. Stir in cherry tomatoes and cook for another minute. In a bowl, whisk eggs, almond milk, garlic powder, black pepper, salt, and oregano.

STEP 2

Pour the egg mixture over the vegetables. Cook for 2–3 minutes until the edges begin to set. Sprinkle with feta cheese (if using). Bake for 10 minutes or until the eggs are fully set.

STEP 3

Remove from the oven and garnish with fresh basil leaves before serving.

NUTRITIONAL INFORMATION

180 Calories, 12g Fat, 8g Carbs, 10g Protein

MAIN DISH

This section presents a thoughtfully curated collection of Mediterranean Diet recipes, designed to be both flavorful and nutritious while supporting overall health and well-being. Each recipe is tailored for two, making it easy to enjoy wholesome meals together. Feel free to adjust ingredients to match your tastes and dietary preferences. If you have specific health concerns or dietary restrictions, consulting a healthcare professional or dietitian can help ensure your meals align with your nutritional goals. Embrace the Mediterranean way of eating and enjoy this delicious journey to better health—one shared meal at a time!

Baked Sea Bass with Salsa

Cooking Difficulty: 3/10	Cooking Time: 31 minutes	Servings: 2

INGREDIENTS

- 2 whole sea bass (each about 1 lb), cleaned and scaled
- 3 tbsp extra virgin olive oil
- Salt and black pepper to taste
- 1 tsp dried oregano
- 1/2 tsp garlic powder
- 1 small lemon, sliced
- 3/4 cup cherry tomatoes, diced
- 3 tbsp black olives, chopped
- 2 tbsp fresh parsley, chopped
- 1 1/2 tbsp fresh lemon juice

DESCRIPTION

STEP 1

Preheat oven to 375°F (190°C). Line a baking sheet with parchment paper.

STEP 2

Rinse the fish, pat dry, and make 2–3 shallow cuts on each side. Rub with olive oil, salt, pepper, oregano, and garlic powder, ensuring the seasoning gets into the cuts. Stuff the cavity of each fish with lemon slices and place them on the baking sheet. Bake for 20–25 minutes, or until the flesh is tender and flakes easily.

STEP 3

Meanwhile, mix tomatoes, olives, parsley, and lemon juice to make the salsa. Once cooked, transfer the fish to a plate and spoon the fresh salsa over the top. Serve immediately.

NUTRITIONAL INFORMATION

340 Calories, 18g Fat, 7g Carbs, 42g Protein

Mediterranean Fish & Lentil Bowl

Cooking Difficulty: 2/10	Cooking Time: 37 minutes	Servings: 2

INGREDIENTS

- 1/2 cup black lentils, rinsed
- 1 1/4 cups water or vegetable broth
- 2 small white fish fillets (such as cod or sea bass)
- 1 tbsp extra virgin olive oil
- Salt and black pepper to taste
- 1/2 tsp dried oregano
- 1/2 tsp garlic powder
- 1/2 cup cherry tomatoes, whole
- 1/4 small red onion, sliced into thin wedges
- 1 tbsp fresh lemon juice
- 1 tbsp fresh parsley, chopped

DESCRIPTION

STEP 1

Cook black lentils in water or broth for 20–25 minutes until tender, then drain.

STEP 2

Preheat oven to 375°F (190°C). Arrange fish, cherry tomatoes, and red onion wedges on a baking sheet. Drizzle with olive oil and season with salt, pepper, oregano, and garlic powder. Roast for 12–15 minutes until the fish is flaky and the vegetables are tender.

STEP 3

Toss cooked lentils with lemon juice and parsley. Serve lentils topped with roasted fish, cherry tomatoes, and red onion.

NUTRITIONAL INFORMATION

350 Calories, 10g Fat, 30g Carbs, 40g Protein

Lemon Capers Chicken Cutlets

Cooking Difficulty: 1/10	Cooking Time: 18 minutes	Servings: 2

INGREDIENTS

- 2 small chicken breasts, pounded thin
- salt and black pepper
- 1 tbsp whole wheat flour
- 1 tbsp olive oil
- 1/2 cup chicken broth
- 2 tbsp lemon juice
- 1 tbsp capers
- 1 tsp lemon zest
- fresh parsley (for garnish)

DESCRIPTION

STEP 1

Season chicken, lightly coat with flour, and sear in olive oil for 3-4 minutes per side. Add broth, lemon juice, capers, and zest. Simmer for 4 minutes. Return chicken to the pan, coat with sauce, and serve garnished with parsley.

NUTRITIONAL INFORMATION

220 Calories, 10g Fat, 2g Carbs, 30g Protein

Baked Chicken with Veggies

Cooking Difficulty: 2/10	Cooking Time: 35 minutes	Servings: 2

INGREDIENTS

- 2 chicken breasts
- 1 cup cherry tomatoes, halved
- 1 cup mushrooms, sliced
- 1 tablespoon olive oil
- 1 teaspoon garlic powder
- 1 teaspoon dried oregano
- salt and pepper to taste
- dried dill (optional)

DESCRIPTION

STEP 1

Preheat the oven to 400°F (200°C). Place chicken breasts on a baking sheet. Drizzle with olive oil, and season with garlic powder, oregano, salt, and pepper. Scatter tomatoes and mushrooms around the chicken. Bake for 20-25 minutes, or until the chicken is cooked through. Serve hot.

NUTRITIONAL INFORMATION

290 Calories, 13g Fat, 10g Carbs, 36g Protein

Scallops with Cauliflower Puree & Asparagus

Cooking Difficulty: 3/10	Cooking Time: 20 minutes	Servings: 2

INGREDIENTS

- 8–10 large scallops, cleaned
- 1 tbsp extra virgin olive oil
- salt and black pepper to taste
- 1/2 head cauliflower, cut into florets
- 1/4 cup unsweetened almond milk
- 1 tbsp fresh lemon juice
- 1 bunch asparagus, trimmed
- 1 tbsp fresh parsley, chopped

DESCRIPTION

STEP 1

Steam cauliflower florets for 10-12 minutes until tender. Drain and blend with almond milk, salt, pepper, and lemon juice until smooth.

STEP 2

While the cauliflower steams, steam the asparagus for 3-4 minutes until tender but crisp.

STEP 3

Heat olive oil in a grill pan or skillet over medium-high heat. Season scallops with salt and pepper and grill for 2–3 minutes per side until golden and cooked through.

STEP 4

Plate the cauliflower puree, top with grilled scallops, and serve with steamed asparagus. Garnish with parsley and serve immediately.

NUTRITIONAL INFORMATION

280 Calories, 15g Fat, 12g Carbs, 30g Protein

Garlic Shrimp with Tomatoes

Cooking Difficulty: 1/10	Cooking Time: 13 minutes	Servings: 2

INGREDIENTS

- 12-14 peeled shrimp
- 1 cup cherry tomatoes (halved)
- 2 cloves garlic (minced)
- 1 tablespoon olive oil
- 1 teaspoon dried oregano
- 1 tablespoon fresh parsley (chopped)
- salt and pepper to taste

DESCRIPTION

STEP 1

Heat olive oil in a skillet over medium heat. Add garlic and sauté for 1 minute until fragrant. Add shrimp and cook for 2-3 minutes on each side until pink and cooked through. Add halved cherry tomatoes and cook for another 2 minutes, until softened. Stir in oregano, parsley, salt, and pepper. Serve and enjoy!

NUTRITIONAL INFORMATION

220 Calories, 12g Fat, 10g Carbs, 25g Protein

Tuna Pasta Salad

Cooking Difficulty: 1/10	Cooking Time: 15 minutes	Servings: 2

INGREDIENTS

- 1 cup whole wheat pasta (cooked and cooled)
- 1/2 red bell pepper (diced)
- 1/4 cup black olives (sliced)
- 1 can (5 oz) tuna in water (drained and flaked)
- 1 tablespoon fresh parsley
- 1 tablespoon olive oil
- 1 teaspoon lemon juice
- salt and pepper to taste

DESCRIPTION

STEP 1

Cook pasta according to package directions, then drain and cool. In a large bowl, combine pasta, bell peppers, olives, and tuna. Add olive oil, lemon juice, parsley, salt, and pepper. Toss to combine. Serve chilled or at room temperature.

NUTRITIONAL INFORMATION

350 Calories, 14g Fat, 35g Carbs, 28g Protein

Salmon Skewers with Couscous

Cooking Difficulty: 3/10	Cooking Time: 27 minutes	Servings: 2

INGREDIENTS

- 2 salmon fillets (cut into chunks)
- 1 medium zucchini (sliced into rounds)
- 1 tablespoon olive oil
- 1 teaspoon lemon zest
- 1 teaspoon dried oregano
- salt and black pepper to taste

for the couscous:

- 1 cup couscous
- 1 tablespoon olive oil
- 1 teaspoon ground cumin
- ½ teaspoon ground cinnamon
- ¼ teaspoon chili flakes (optional for heat)
- ½ cup pomegranate seeds
- ¼ cup fresh parsley (chopped)
- salt and black pepper to taste

DESCRIPTION

STEP 1

Preheat the grill to medium-high. Thread salmon chunks and zucchini slices onto skewers. Brush with olive oil, lemon zest, oregano, salt, and pepper. Grill the skewers for 10-12 minutes, turning occasionally, until the salmon is cooked through.

STEP 2

For the couscous: Heat olive oil in a pan, add cumin, cinnamon, and chili flakes, and toast for 1-2 minutes. Add couscous and boiling water, cover, and let it steam for 5 minutes. Fluff with a fork.

STEP 3

Stir in pomegranate seeds, parsley, salt, and pepper. Serve the skewers over the couscous.

NUTRITIONAL INFORMATION

420 Calories, 18g Fat, 35g Carbs, 35g Protein

Spicy Grilled Cauliflower Steaks

Cooking Difficulty: 1/10	Cooking Time: 25 minutes	Servings: 2

INGREDIENTS

- 1 medium cauliflower head (cut into 2 thick steaks)
- 2 tablespoons olive oil
- 1 teaspoon chili flakes
- 1 teaspoon fresh parsley
- 1 teaspoon fresh cilantro
- 1/2 teaspoon garlic powder
- salt and pepper to taste

DESCRIPTION

STEP 1

Preheat grill to medium-high heat. Brush cauliflower steaks with 1 tablespoon olive oil, season with salt and pepper, and grill for 6-7 minutes per side. Mix remaining olive oil with chili flakes, garlic powder, parsley, cilantro, salt, and pepper. Drizzle over grilled cauliflower steaks and serve.

NUTRITIONAL INFORMATION

180 Calories, 14g Fat, 12g Carbs, 4g Protein

Lentil Patties

Cooking Difficulty: 2/10	Cooking Time: 30 minutes	Servings: 2

INGREDIENTS

- 1 cup cooked lentils
- 1/4 cup breadcrumbs
- 1/4 cup grated carrot
- 1 tablespoon fresh parsley
- 1 tablespoon olive oil
- 1 teaspoon garlic powder
- 1/2 teaspoon cumin
- salt and pepper to taste

DESCRIPTION

STEP 1

In a bowl, mash the cooked lentils. Add breadcrumbs, grated carrot, parsley, olive oil, garlic powder, cumin, salt, and pepper. Mix well.Form the mixture into small patties. Heat olive oil in a pan and cook patties for 3-4 minutes on each side until golden brown. Serve with your favorite salad.

NUTRITIONAL INFORMATION

230 Calories, 8g Fat, 30g Carbs, 12g Protein

Mediterranean Chicken Drumsticks

Cooking Difficulty: 2/10	Cooking Time: 50 minutes	Servings: 4

INGREDIENTS

- 4 chicken drumsticks (thigh and leg pieces)
- 2 tablespoons olive oil
- 2 teaspoons fresh rosemary (chopped)
- 2 teaspoons fresh thyme (chopped)
- 1 teaspoon fresh sage (chopped)
- 1 teaspoon garlic powder
- 1 teaspoon onion powder
- ½ teaspoon smoked paprika
- salt and black pepper to taste
- 1 lemon (cut into wedges)

DESCRIPTION

STEP 1

Preheat the oven to 400°F (200°C).

STEP 2

In a small bowl, mix olive oil, rosemary, thyme, sage, garlic powder, onion powder, smoked paprika, salt, and pepper. Rub the herb mixture evenly over the chicken drumsticks.

STEP 3

Place the drumsticks on a baking sheet lined with parchment paper.Squeeze half a lemon over the drumsticks, and place the lemon wedges around the chicken. Bake for 35-40 minutes, or until the drumsticks reach an internal temperature of 165°F (75°C) and the skin is crispy. Serve with your favorite side dish or salad.

NUTRITIONAL INFORMATION

320 Calories, 22g Fat, 2g Carbs, 28g Protein

Fish & Veggie Patties

Cooking Difficulty: 1/10	Cooking Time: 25 minutes	Servings: 2

INGREDIENTS

- 1/2 lb salmon, finely chopped
- 1/2 cup broccoli florets, chopped
- 1/2 cup grated carrot
- 1/4 cup breadcrumbs
- 1 tablespoon olive oil
- 1 teaspoon garlic powder
- 1/2 teaspoon dried dill
- salt and pepper to taste

DESCRIPTION

STEP 1

Preheat the oven to 375°F (190°C). Combine fish, broccoli, carrot, breadcrumbs, garlic powder, dill, salt, and pepper. Form patties and place on a lined baking sheet. Drizzle with olive oil and bake for 15-20 minutes. Serve with your favorite side.

NUTRITIONAL INFORMATION

250 Calories, 14g Fat, 12g Carbs, 20g Protein

Cabbage Steak

Cooking Difficulty: 1/10	Cooking Time: 22 minutes	Servings: 2

INGREDIENTS

- 1/2 head of cabbage, sliced into 1-inch thick steaks
- 1 tablespoon olive oil
- 1 teaspoon garlic powder
- 1/2 teaspoon smoked paprika
- 1 teaspoons thyme (chopped)
- salt and pepper to taste

DESCRIPTION

STEP 1

Preheat oven to 400°F (200°C). Drizzle cabbage steaks with olive oil and season with garlic powder, paprika, thyme, salt, and pepper. Place on a baking sheet and roast for 20 minutes, flipping halfway through. Serve hot with your favorite sauce.

NUTRITIONAL INFORMATION

120 Calories, 8g Fat, 10g Carbs, 2g Protein

Garlic Herb Stuffed Langoustines

Cooking Difficulty: 1/10	Cooking Time: 25 minutes	Servings: 2

INGREDIENTS

- 10 large langoustines (split along the back)
- 3 tablespoons olive oil
- 4 cloves garlic (minced)
- 3 tablespoons fresh parsley (chopped)
- 2 tablespoons fresh basil (chopped)
- 1 teaspoon lemon zest
- 1 teaspoon smoked paprika
- salt and black pepper to taste
- 1 ½ tablespoons lemon juice

DESCRIPTION

STEP 1

Preheat oven to 400°F (200°C).

STEP 2

In a bowl, mix garlic, parsley, basil, lemon zest, smoked paprika, salt, and pepper with olive oil. Stuff the mixture into the split backs of the langoustines.

STEP 3

Arrange langoustines on a baking sheet and bake for 12-15 minutes until pink and cooked through.

STEP 4

Drizzle with lemon juice and serve with your favorite salad greens. A delicious, protein-packed seafood dish with bold flavors!

NUTRITIONAL INFORMATION

340 Calories, 14g Fat, 4g Carbs, 48g Protein

Spiced Fish & Sweet Potato Fries

Cooking Difficulty: 3/10	Cooking Time: 40 minutes	Servings: 2

INGREDIENTS

- 2 white fish fillets (such as cod, haddock, or tilapia)
- 1 tablespoon olive oil
- 1 teaspoon paprika
- 1 teaspoon garlic powder
- 1 teaspoon lemon zest
- ½ teaspoon dried oregano
- salt and black pepper to taste
- 1 medium sweet potato (cut into thin fries)
- 1 tablespoon olive oil (for sweet potato fries)
- 1 teaspoon smoked paprika (for sweet potato fries)
- 1 tablespoon fresh lemon juice

DESCRIPTION

STEP 1

Preheat the oven to 400°F (200°C). Toss the sweet potato fries with olive oil, smoked paprika, salt, and pepper. Spread them on a baking sheet in a single layer and bake for 20-25 minutes, flipping halfway through, until crispy.

STEP 2

Meanwhile, rub the white fish fillets with olive oil, paprika, garlic powder, lemon zest, oregano, salt, and pepper. Place the fish fillets on a separate baking sheet and bake for 12-15 minutes, or until the fish flakes easily with a fork.

STEP 3

Serve the baked fish with the sweet potato fries, and drizzle with fresh lemon juice before serving.

NUTRITIONAL INFORMATION

350 Calories, 12g Fat, 40g Carbs, 30g Protein

Spiced Chicken Drumsticks

Cooking Difficulty: 1/10	Cooking Time: 50 minutes	Servings: 4

INGREDIENTS

- 8 chicken drumsticks
- 1 tablespoon olive oil
- 1 teaspoon chili powder
- 1 teaspoon cumin
- 1 teaspoon paprika
- 1/2 teaspoon garlic powder
- 1/2 teaspoon onion powder
- salt and pepper to taste

DESCRIPTION

STEP 1

Preheat oven to 400°F (200°C). Toss chicken drumsticks with olive oil and spices. Arrange drumsticks on a baking sheet and bake for 35-40 minutes, or until cooked through and crispy. Serve hot with your favorite salad.

NUTRITIONAL INFORMATION

250 Calories, 15g Fat, 3g Carbs, 28g Protein

Zucchini & Chickpea Bake

Cooking Difficulty: 1/10	Cooking Time: 32 minutes	Servings: 2

INGREDIENTS

- 2 medium zucchinis, sliced into rings
- 1 cup canned chickpeas, drained and rinsed
- 2 medium sweet potatoes, sliced
- 1 tablespoon olive oil
- 1 teaspoon paprika
- 1/2 teaspoon garlic powder

DESCRIPTION

STEP 1

Preheat oven to 400°F (200°C). Toss zucchini rings, chickpeas, and sweet potato slices with olive oil, paprika, garlic powder, salt, and pepper. Spread evenly on a baking sheet and bake for 20-25 minutes, flipping halfway, until tender and golden. Serve.

NUTRITIONAL INFORMATION

180 Calories, 7g Fat, 32g Carbs, 6g Protein

Grilled Salmon over Mediterranean Salad

Cooking Difficulty: 2/10	Cooking Time: 20 minutes	Servings: 2

INGREDIENTS

- 2 fillets of salmon (about 4 oz each)
- 1 tablespoon olive oil
- ½ teaspoon dried oregano
- ½ teaspoon garlic powder
- salt and pepper to taste

for the salad:

- 2 cups mixed salad greens
- ½ cup cherry tomatoes
- ¼ cup black olives (sliced)
- ½ cup cooked green beans
- 2 boiled eggs (cut into 6 wedges each)

for the dressing:

- 2 tablespoons extra virgin olive oil
- 1 tablespoon fresh lemon juice
- 1 teaspoon dijon mustard
- 1 small garlic clove (minced)
- salt and pepper to taste

DESCRIPTION

STEP 1

Preheat the grill to medium heat. Rub salmon with olive oil, oregano, garlic powder, salt, and pepper. Grill for about 4-5 minutes per side until cooked through.

STEP 2

In a small bowl, whisk together all dressing ingredients. Arrange salad greens, cherry tomatoes, olives, green beans, and boiled egg wedges on a plate.

STEP 3

Place grilled salmon on top and drizzle with the dressing. Serve immediately!

NUTRITIONAL INFORMATION

400 Calories, 25g Fat, 12g Carbs, 35g Protein

Bulgur Salad with Raisins & Veggies

Cooking Difficulty: 2/10	Cooking Time: 21 minutes	Servings: 2

INGREDIENTS

- 1/2 cup bulgur
- 1/2 cup boiling water
- 1/2 cup cherry tomatoes, halved
- 1/2 cucumber, diced
- 1/4 cup raisins
- 1/2 cup mixed greens (such as arugula or spinach)
- 1 tbsp extra virgin olive oil
- 1 tbsp lemon juice
- 1 tsp honey
- 1/2 tsp cumin
- salt and black pepper to taste

DESCRIPTION

STEP 1

lace bulgur in a bowl and pour boiling water over it. Cover the bowl and let the bulgur steam for about 10-12 minutes, or until it absorbs all the water and softens.

STEP 2

While the bulgur is steaming, prepare the vegetables and greens. Slice the cherry tomatoes in half, dice the cucumber, and roughly chop the mixed greens.

STEP 3

In a small bowl, whisk together the olive oil, lemon juice, honey, cumin, salt, and pepper to create the dressing. Once the bulgur is ready, combine it with the tomatoes, cucumber, raisins, and greens in a large bowl. Drizzle the dressing over the salad and toss gently to combine.

NUTRITIONAL INFORMATION

250 Calories, 10g Fat, 35g Carbs, 6g Protein

Leek Cream Soup

Cooking Difficulty: 1/10	Cooking Time: 25 minutes	Servings: 2

INGREDIENTS

- 1 leek, chopped
- 2 cups cauliflower florets
- 2 cups vegetable broth
- 1 tablespoon olive oil
- 1 teaspoon garlic powder
- salt and pepper to taste

DESCRIPTION

STEP 1

In a large pot, heat olive oil over medium heat. Add leek and sauté for 3-4 minutes until softened. Add cauliflower florets, garlic powder, salt, and pepper. Stir well. Pour in the vegetable broth and bring to a simmer. Cook for about 15 minutes, or until cauliflower is tender. Using an immersion blender, blend the soup until smooth and creamy. Serve hot.

NUTRITIONAL INFORMATION

130 Calories, 6g Fat, 18g Carbs, 4g Protein

Zucchini Cream Soup

Cooking Difficulty: 1/10	Cooking Time: 25 minutes	Servings: 2

INGREDIENTS

- 2 medium zucchinis, chopped
- 1 small onion, chopped
- 1 tablespoon olive oil
- 2 cups vegetable broth
- 1/2 cup coconut milk (or preferred milk for the diet)
- salt and pepper to taste
- fresh herbs (optional, for garnish)

DESCRIPTION

STEP 1

Sauté onion in olive oil until soft. Add zucchini and broth, cook until tender. Remove from heat and blend the soup until smooth using an immersion blender or regular blender. Stir in coconut milk, season with salt and pepper, and heat through. Serve hot!

NUTRITIONAL INFORMATION

160 Calories, 10g Fat, 16g Carbs, 3g Protein

Greek Chicken Skewers with Tzatziki

Cooking Difficulty: 3/10	Cooking Time: 25 minutes	Servings: 2

INGREDIENTS

- 2 chicken breasts, cut into cubes
- 1 tbsp olive oil
- 1 tsp dried oregano
- salt and black pepper to taste
- 2 whole wheat pita breads
- 1/2 cucumber, sliced
- 1/4 cup black olives, pitted and sliced
- 1/4 cup feta cheese, crumbled
- fresh parsley or mint for garnish

for the tzatziki sauce:

- 1/2 cup Greek yogurt
- 1/2 cucumber, grated and drained
- 1 tbsp olive oil
- 1 tbsp lemon juice
- 1 tsp garlic, minced
- salt and pepper to taste

DESCRIPTION

STEP 1

Toss chicken cubes with olive oil, oregano, salt, and pepper. Thread onto skewers. Grill the chicken for 4–5 minutes per side until cooked through.

STEP 2

Mix Greek yogurt, grated cucumber, olive oil, lemon juice, garlic, salt, and pepper for the tzatziki sauce.

STEP 3

Warm the pita breads, then arrange them on plates.

STEP 4

Place chicken skewers on the pita, top with cucumber, olives, feta, and tzatziki. Garnish with fresh herbs and serve immediately.

NUTRITIONAL INFORMATION

400 Calories, 18g Fat, 30g Carbs, 35g Protein

Arugula Pear & Blue Cheese Salad

Cooking Difficulty: 1/10	Cooking Time: 5 minutes	Servings: 2

INGREDIENTS

- 2 cups arugula
- 1/4 cup blue cheese, crumbled
- 1/2 pear, sliced
- 1/2 cup red or green grapes, halved
- 2 tbsp mixed nuts (walnuts or almonds), roughly chopped
- 1 tbsp extra virgin olive oil
- 1 tbsp balsamic vinegar
- salt and pepper to taste

DESCRIPTION

STEP 1

In a large bowl, combine the arugula, blue cheese, pear slices, and grapes. In a small bowl, whisk together olive oil, balsamic vinegar, salt, and pepper. Drizzle the dressing over the salad and toss gently. Sprinkle with chopped nuts and serve immediately.

NUTRITIONAL INFORMATION

300 Calories, 20g Fat, 15g Carbs, 6g Protein

Mediterranean Arugula Salad

Cooking Difficulty: 1/10	Cooking Time: 8 minutes	Servings: 2

INGREDIENTS

- 2 cups arugula
- 1/4 cup black olives, sliced
- 1/2 red bell pepper, thinly sliced
- 1/2 cucumber, sliced
- 1/2 cup cherry tomatoes, halved
- 1 boiled egg, sliced
- 1/4 cup torn mozzarella cheese
- 1 tbsp olive oil
- 1 tbsp lemon juice
- salt and pepper to taste

DESCRIPTION

STEP 1

In a large bowl, combine the arugula, olives, red pepper, cucumber, cherry tomatoes, and boiled egg. Tear the mozzarella into pieces and add it to the salad. Drizzle with olive oil and lemon juice, then season with salt and pepper. Serve immediately.

NUTRITIONAL INFORMATION

300 Calories, 22g Fat, 15g Carbs, 15g Protein

Herb-Baked Mackerel with Chickpeas

Cooking Difficulty: 2/10	Cooking Time: 30 minutes	Servings: 2

INGREDIENTS

- 2 mackerel fillets
- 1 tbsp extra virgin olive oil
- 1 tsp dried thyme
- 1/2 tsp garlic powder
- salt and black pepper to taste
- 1/2 cup cherry tomatoes, whole
- 1/2 cup cooked chickpeas (or canned, drained and rinsed)
- 1 tbsp fresh lemon juice
- fresh parsley for garnish

DESCRIPTION

STEP 1

Preheat oven to 375°F (190°C).

STEP 2

Place the mackerel fillets on a baking sheet, drizzle with olive oil, and season with thyme, garlic powder, salt, and pepper. Add cherry tomatoes and chickpeas around the fish on the baking sheet.

STEP 3

Bake for 20-25 minutes or until the fish is cooked through and flakes easily with a fork.

STEP 4

Drizzle with fresh lemon juice and garnish with parsley. Serve immediately.

NUTRITIONAL INFORMATION

400 Calories, 20g Fat, 25g Carbs, 35g Protein

Grilled Zucchini & Burrata Salad

Cooking Difficulty: 1/10	Cooking Time: 10 minutes	Servings: 2

INGREDIENTS

- 1 medium zucchini, sliced
- 1 tbsp olive oil
- salt and pepper to taste
- 1/2 cup cherry tomatoes, halved
- 1/4 cup black olives, pitted and sliced
- 1 ball burrata, torn into pieces
- fresh basil leaves for garnish

DESCRIPTION

STEP 1

Preheat the grill or grill pan over medium heat. Drizzle zucchini slices with olive oil and season with salt and pepper. Grill for 2–3 minutes per side until tender and slightly charred. Arrange grilled zucchini, cherry tomatoes, olives, and burrata on a plate. Garnish with fresh basil and serve immediately.

NUTRITIONAL INFORMATION

250 Calories, 20g Fat, 10g Carbs, 12g Protein

Shrimp & Avocado Salad

Cooking Difficulty: 1/10	Cooking Time: 5 minutes	Servings: 2

INGREDIENTS

- 12 large shrimp, cooked and peeled
- 1 avocado, diced
- 1/4 red onion, finely chopped
- 2 cups arugula
- 1 tbsp olive oil
- 1 tbsp lemon juice
- salt and pepper to taste

DESCRIPTION

STEP 1

In a large bowl, combine the shrimp, avocado, red onion, and arugula. Drizzle with olive oil and lemon juice, then season with salt and pepper. Toss gently to combine and serve immediately.

NUTRITIONAL INFORMATION

300 Calories, 20g Fat, 10g Carbs, 25g Protein

Tomato-Braised Chicken with Peppers

Cooking Difficulty: 3/10	Cooking Time: 35 minutes	Servings: 4

INGREDIENTS

- 1 lb boneless, skinless chicken thighs (cut into cubes)
- 1 red bell pepper (sliced)
- 1 yellow bell pepper (sliced)
- 1 green bell pepper (sliced)
- 1 small onion (chopped)
- 2 cloves garlic (minced)
- 1 cup crushed tomatoes
- ½ cup chicken broth
- 1 tablespoon olive oil
- ½ teaspoon smoked paprika
- ½ teaspoon dried oregano
- ¼ teaspoon ground cumin
- salt and pepper to taste

DESCRIPTION

STEP 1

Heat olive oil in a large pan over medium heat. Add chicken and cook until browned. Remove and set aside.

STEP 2

In the same pan, sauté onion and garlic until fragrant. Add bell peppers and cook for 3 minutes. Stir in crushed tomatoes, chicken broth, paprika, oregano, cumin, salt, and pepper. Return chicken to the pan. Cover and simmer for 15-20 minutes until the chicken is tender.

STEP 3

Serve with your favorite side dish and enjoy!

NUTRITIONAL INFORMATION

250 Calories, 10g Fat, 12g Carbs, 28g Protein

Stewed Vegetables with White Beans

Cooking Difficulty: 2/10	Cooking Time: 33 minutes	Servings: 2

INGREDIENTS

- 1 tbsp olive oil
- 1 small zucchini, diced
- 1 small eggplant, diced
- 1/2 red bell pepper, diced
- 1/2 yellow bell pepper, diced
- 1/2 green bell pepper, diced
- 1/2 onion, diced
- 2 garlic cloves, minced
- 1/2 cup cooked white beans (or canned, drained and rinsed)
- 1 cup vegetable broth
- 1/2 tsp dried thyme
- 1/2 tsp dried oregano
- salt and black pepper to taste
- fresh parsley for garnish

DESCRIPTION

STEP 1

Heat olive oil in a large pot over medium heat. Add onion, garlic, zucchini, eggplant, and bell peppers. Cook for 5–7 minutes until vegetables start to soften.

STEP 2

Add vegetable broth, white beans, thyme, oregano, salt, and pepper. Bring to a simmer. Cover and cook for 15–20 minutes, stirring occasionally, until vegetables are tender and flavors have melded together.

STEP 3

Garnish with fresh parsley and serve immediately.

NUTRITIONAL INFORMATION

250 Calories, 10g Fat, 30g Carbs, 10g Protein

SNACKS & DESSERTS

This section presents a thoughtfully curated collection of Mediterranean Diet recipes, designed to be both flavorful and nutritious while supporting overall health and well-being. Each recipe is tailored for two, making it easy to enjoy wholesome meals together. Feel free to adjust ingredients to match your tastes and dietary preferences. If you have specific health concerns or dietary restrictions, consulting a healthcare professional or dietitian can help ensure your meals align with your nutritional goals. Embrace the Mediterranean way of eating and enjoy this delicious journey to better health—one shared meal at a time!

Falafel with Hummus

Cooking Difficulty: 3/10	Cooking Time: 25 minutes	Servings: 2

INGREDIENTS

- 1 cup canned chickpeas (drained and rinsed)
- 1 garlic clove (minced)
- 2 tablespoons chopped parsley
- ½ teaspoon cumin
- ¼ teaspoon black pepper
- 1 tablespoon olive oil

for the hummus:

- ½ cup canned chickpeas
- 1 tablespoon tahini
- 1 teaspoon lemon juice
- 1 teaspoon olive oil
- ¼ teaspoon garlic powder

DESCRIPTION

STEP 1

In a food processor, combine chickpeas, garlic, parsley, cumin, and black pepper. Blend until the mixture is slightly coarse but holds together when pressed. Form into small patties. Heat olive oil in a pan over medium heat. Add falafel patties and cook for about 3–4 minutes per side until golden and crispy. Remove from heat and set aside.

STEP 2

For the hummus, blend chickpeas, tahini, lemon juice, olive oil, and garlic powder until smooth. Add a little water if needed to reach the desired consistency.

STEP 3

Serve the falafel warm with hummus on the side. Enjoy!

NUTRITIONAL INFORMATION

350 Calories, 16g Fat, 40g Carbs, 12g Protein

Stuffed Figs with Nuts & Blue Cheese

Cooking Difficulty: 1/10	Cooking Time: 12 minutes	Servings: 2

INGREDIENTS

- 6 fresh figs, halved
- 1/4 cup walnuts or pecans, chopped
- 2 tbsp blue cheese, crumbled
- 1 tsp honey (optional)
- fresh thyme for garnish (optional)

DESCRIPTION

STEP 1

Preheat the oven to 375°F (190°C). Scoop out a small portion from each fig half. Stuff with chopped nuts and blue cheese. Place on a baking sheet and bake for 8–10 minutes until figs are tender and cheese melts. Drizzle with honey and garnish with thyme, if desired. Serve immediately.

NUTRITIONAL INFORMATION

200 Calories, 16g Fat, 18g Carbs, 4g Protein

Chocolate Panna Cotta

Cooking Difficulty: 1/10	Cooking Time: 10 minutes	Servings: 2

INGREDIENTS

- 1 cup heavy cream
- 1/2 cup unsweetened almond milk
- 2 oz dark chocolate (70% cocoa or higher), chopped
- 1 tbsp honey or maple syrup (optional)
- 1 tsp vanilla extract
- 1 tsp gelatin (optional)

DESCRIPTION

STEP 1

Heat heavy cream and almond milk in a saucepan until simmering. Remove from heat, stir in chopped chocolate until smooth. Add honey, vanilla, and dissolve gelatin (if using). Pour into cups and refrigerate for 4 hours or until set. Serve chilled with berries or cocoa powder, if desired.

NUTRITIONAL INFORMATION

250 Calories, 22g Fat, 15g Carbs, 3g Protein

Baked Artichoke Halves

Cooking Difficulty: 1/10	Cooking Time: 40 minutes	Servings: 2

INGREDIENTS

- 2 large artichokes, halved and cleaned
- 2 tbsp olive oil
- 2 garlic cloves, minced
- 1 tbsp lemon juice
- Salt and pepper to taste
- 1 tbsp fresh parsley, chopped

DESCRIPTION

STEP 1
Preheat the oven to 375°F (190°C).

STEP 2
Cut the artichokes in half and remove the choke (the fuzzy part).

STEP 3
Place artichoke halves on a baking sheet, drizzle with olive oil, lemon juice, garlic, salt, and pepper. Bake for 30-35 minutes, or until the artichokes are tender and golden.

STEP 3
Garnish with fresh parsley and serve immediately.

NUTRITIONAL INFORMATION

150 Calories, 12g Fat, 14g Carbs, 4g Protein

Carrot-Peach Chia Smoothie

Cooking Difficulty: 1/10	Cooking Time: 5 minutes	Servings: 2

INGREDIENTS

- 1 medium carrot (chopped)
- 1 ripe pear (cored and chopped)
- 1 ripe peach (chopped)
- ½ frozen banana
- 1 cup unsweetened almond milk
- ½ teaspoon ground cinnamon
- ½ teaspoon fresh ginger (grated)
- 1 teaspoon honey or maple syrup (optional)
- 1 tablespoon chia seeds

DESCRIPTION

STEP 1

Blend all ingredients (except chia seeds) until smooth. Pour into glasses and sprinkle with chia seeds. Serve immediately and enjoy!

NUTRITIONAL INFORMATION

150 Calories, 3g Fat, 32g Carbs, 3g Protein

Spiced Roasted Baby Carrots

Cooking Difficulty: 1/10	Cooking Time: 25 minutes	Servings: 2

INGREDIENTS

- 2 cups baby carrots
- 1 tablespoon olive oil
- ½ teaspoon smoked paprika
- ½ teaspoon ground cumin
- ¼ teaspoon cinnamon
- salt and pepper to taste

DESCRIPTION

STEP 1

Preheat the oven to 400°F (200°C). Toss baby carrots with olive oil, smoked paprika, cumin, cinnamon, salt, and pepper. Spread on a baking sheet and roast for 18-20 minutes until tender and slightly caramelized. Serve warm with your favorite sauce. A delicious and healthy snack with a hint of spice!

NUTRITIONAL INFORMATION

120 Calories, 5g Fat, 14g Carbs, 1g Protein

Baked Eggplant Parmesan

Cooking Difficulty: 2/10	Cooking Time: 45 minutes	Servings: 2

INGREDIENTS

- 2 medium eggplants, sliced into 1/2-inch rounds
- 1 cup marinara sauce (preferably homemade or low-sugar)
- 1/2 cup mozzarella cheese, shredded
- 1/4 cup parmesan cheese, grated
- 2 tbsp olive oil
- 1 tbsp dried oregano
- salt and pepper to taste
- fresh basil leaves for garnish

DESCRIPTION

STEP 1

Preheat the oven to 375°F (190°C). Brush the eggplant slices with olive oil, season with salt, pepper, and oregano. Place them on a baking sheet and bake for 20 minutes, flipping halfway through.

STEP 2

In a baking dish, spread a thin layer of marinara sauce. Layer the baked eggplant slices, followed by a spoonful of marinara sauce, mozzarella, and Parmesan cheese. Repeat the layers.

STEP 3

Bake for 15–20 minutes until the cheese is melted and bubbly. Garnish with fresh basil and serve immediately.

NUTRITIONAL INFORMATION

250 Calories, 20g Fat, 15g Carbs, 12g Protein

Cauliflower Bites with Red Sauce

Cooking Difficulty: 1/10	Cooking Time: 15 minutes	Servings: 2

INGREDIENTS

- 2 cups cauliflower florets
- 1 tablespoon olive oil
- salt and pepper to taste
- 2 tablespoons marinara sauce
- 1 teaspoon hot sauce (optional, for spice)
- ½ teaspoon balsamic vinegar

DESCRIPTION

STEP 1

Heat olive oil in a pan over medium heat. Add cauliflower florets, season with salt and pepper, and sauté for 8–10 minutes until tender. In a bowl, mix marinara sauce, hot sauce, balsamic vinegar, and garlic powder. Pour the sauce over the cooked cauliflower and stir to coat evenly. Serve warm and enjoy!

NUTRITIONAL INFORMATION

140 Calories, 7g Fat, 15g Carbs, 4g Protein

Spiced Nuts

Cooking Difficulty: 1/10	Cooking Time: 15 minutes	Servings: 4

INGREDIENTS

- 1 cup mixed nuts (walnuts, almonds, pecans)
- 1 tablespoon olive oil
- ½ teaspoon smoked paprika
- ½ teaspoon ground cinnamon
- ¼ teaspoon cayenne pepper
- ½ teaspoon sea salt
- 1 teaspoon honey or maple syrup

DESCRIPTION

STEP 1

Preheat the oven to 350°F (175°C). In a bowl, mix nuts with olive oil, smoked paprika, cinnamon, cayenne (if using), salt, and honey. Spread the nuts on a baking sheet in a single layer. Roast for 8-10 minutes, stirring once, until fragrant and golden. Let cool and enjoy!

NUTRITIONAL INFORMATION

180 Calories, 16g Fat, 7g Carbs, 4g Protein

Almond-Crusted Green Beans

Cooking Difficulty: 2/10	Cooking Time: 20 minutes	Servings: 2

INGREDIENTS

- 2 cups fresh green beans (trimmed)
- ¼ cup almonds (finely chopped)
- 1 tablespoon whole wheat breadcrumbs
- 1 tablespoon olive oil
- ¼ teaspoon black pepper
- ¼ teaspoon garlic powder

DESCRIPTION

STEP 1

Preheat oven to 375°F (190°C). Line a baking sheet with parchment paper.

STEP 2

In a bowl, mix chopped almonds, breadcrumbs, black pepper, and garlic powder. Toss green beans with olive oil, then coat them with the almond mixture. Spread green beans on the baking sheet and bake for 12–15 minutes until crispy.

STEP 3

Serve warm as a healthy side dish. A delicious, crunchy way to enjoy brain-friendly green beans!

NUTRITIONAL INFORMATION

180 Calories, 12g Fat, 14g Carbs, 5g Protein

Spicy Caramelized Bananas

Cooking Difficulty: 1/10	Cooking Time: 20 minutes	Servings: 2

INGREDIENTS

- 2 ripe bananas (sliced)
- 1 tablespoon coconut oil
- 1 tablespoon honey (or maple syrup)
- ½ teaspoon ground cinnamon
- ¼ teaspoon cayenne pepper (optional, for heat)
- pinch of salt

DESCRIPTION

STEP 1

Heat coconut oil in a pan over medium heat. Add banana slices to the pan and cook for 2-3 minutes on each side until golden and caramelized. In a small bowl, mix honey, cinnamon, cayenne pepper, and a pinch of salt. Drizzle the spiced caramel sauce over the bananas and cook for an additional 1 minute.

NUTRITIONAL INFORMATION

150 Calories, 7g Fat, 40g Carbs, 1g Protein

Roasted Quince Stuffed with Nuts

Cooking Difficulty: 1/10	Cooking Time: 35 minutes	Servings: 2

INGREDIENTS

- 2 quinces (peeled, cored, and halved)
- 1 tablespoon olive oil
- ¼ cup mixed nuts
- 1 tablespoon honey
- ½ teaspoon cinnamon
- pinch of salt

DESCRIPTION

STEP 1

Preheat the oven to 375°F (190°C). Place the quince halves in a baking dish, drizzle with olive oil, and sprinkle with a pinch of salt. In a small bowl, mix chopped nuts, honey, and cinnamon. Stuff the quince halves with the nut mixture and cover with foil. Roast for 25-30 minutes, until the quinces are tender and caramelized. Serve and enjoy!

NUTRITIONAL INFORMATION

220 Calories, 12g Fat, 30g Carbs, 4g Protein

Conclusion

The Mediterranean Diet is more than just a way of eating—it's a lifestyle that nurtures health, enhances well-being, and brings people together. By embracing fresh, whole foods, heart-healthy fats, and mindful eating habits, you and your partner can enjoy delicious meals while reaping the benefits of better digestion, improved heart health, sustainable weight loss, and overall vitality.

Cooking and dining together not only strengthens your health but also deepens your connection, turning mealtime into a shared experience of joy and wellness. With its balance of nutrition, flavor, and simplicity, the Mediterranean way of life is easy to sustain, making healthy eating enjoyable rather than restrictive.

As you continue this journey, remember that the best diet is the one that fits seamlessly into your lifestyle. Savor each meal, stay active, and embrace the Mediterranean philosophy of balance and togetherness. Wishing you a lifetime of health, happiness, and delicious meals for two!

Alan Caplan

Printed in Dunstable, United Kingdom

63559630R00058